Delicious
Silence

poems from
the tiger's mouth

by
Chris McCombs

FANA PRESS

Delicious Silence
poems from the tiger's mouth

For information address: Fana Press
Post Office Box 667, Eastsound, Washington 98245-0667

Published by
Fana Press
Post Office Box 667, Eastsound, Washington 98245-0667
(360) 376-7601   (fana@rockisland.com)

Painting of Ramana Maharshi
by
Spar Street at Ra Vision
667 Baycrest Drive, North Vancouver, BC Canada
(604) 924-0444

Printed in the United States of America.

Library of Congress Catalog Card Number 99-97742

ISBN 1-893486-08-7

Dedicated to

Gangaji

and

the

silence

Contents

Foreword

By Gangaji

When Chris first read his poetry at a retreat,
the room of over 300 people became electrified.
We were thrilled to hear
the outpouring of the awakened heart.

Somehow he manages the impossible task
all great artists and mystics share— the articulation of
the supreme mystery which forever evades capture.

Poetry is, of course, our only hope
in verbal articulation of the mystery,
which is both linear and circular.

There is a resolution in Chris' poetry that leaves one
reveling in certain and drunken knowing
while falling deeper into the ungraspable,
unknowable realm.
The mind is slain as the spirit soars.

I invite you into his heart's expression
that you may taste it for yourself.

Introduction

These poems were written during an intense period

of awakening that followed the Cobb Mountain

seven-day silent retreat with Gangaji in April of 1998.

The silence was so profound, so enduring . . .

I was captured completely.

My head had been in the tiger's mouth* for years.

But at the retreat, I was swallowed by the silence.

And in the months that followed . . . digested!

The Sufis call the process "fana," annihilation in God.

It is the most delicious disappearing act.

Who you thought you were gives way to a

knowing yourself as awareness itself,

at the core of everything.

These poems carry the flavor of that disappearance,

like sugar dissolving in water.

* The "tiger" is a metaphor for The Self, Buddha Nature, that which you
"awaken to" as the ego dissolves. When the longing for God arises within you, your head
goes into the tiger's mouth.

Notes

Raise Your Anchor

A fresh wind
Is blowing . . .
Hoist your sails

Don't forget
To raise the anchor

All adventures
Require letting go of something

Notes

The Tavern

We have all been drinking
At the same tavern

Now drunk
On the deep red wine
That only the Heart
Can make

We have been bathing
In that pool
But no one is getting wet

We have been
Passing the cup around
But it is only getting fuller

Sacred letters are written
On its rim
But no one is left
To read them

Just the drinking
And the drowning

Notes

This Love Says
Whatever It Wants

This love
Says whatever it wants
And I don't get
In the way

She loves it all
And revels in the saying
Of it

Adoring this one
Praising that one
Laughing Herself silly

When I return
To the house
I am embarrassed
By the lavishness of the feast

The unabashed praising
The wild singing
Flowers everywhere

She says:
Don't close the door
And lock it behind you

Blow the wall away . . . instead

Notes

Gate Keeper

Every soul
Has a gate keeper
You are that!

The gate keeper's job?
To hold the gates open
So the soul
Can experience the world

Raise your hand
Answer . . . present!

If you wander off
With every beggar
The gates close
And your soul weeps

It longs for your presence

Every thought is a beggar
Passing by the gates
If you pay attention to them
You wander off in their company

What sane man
Would accompany beggars
When the Divine Lover
Waits alone in his chest

Continued

Notes

Stay at your post
In the present moment
Empty of all thought

Your soul will reward you
With the joy of its Being

Notes

The Student & The Sage

What is the difference
Between a student
And a sage?

The sage dwells
In the stillness
Of his original nature

The student
Still thinks
There is something
To think about

Notes

Drink This

I checked the box
Called ecstatic poet

Drinking You in
I become drunk
With Your love
Aflame with Your presence

I, a personality
Seeking its own True Nature
You, the True Nature
Seeking to awaken Your personality

Let's get drunk together

The pearls are here in my mouth
Only You can speak them

Notes

The Goddess Was Here Last Night

The Goddess
Was here last night
I can feel it

Earrings on the couch
Nail polish in the corner

Sacred singing
And ecstatic dancing
Linger

Her perfume
Still here in the chest

Her scent
Is a wild praising
Of life

Notes

Finish Me Off

Finish me off!
This going back and forth
Across the threshold
Is driving me crazy

Empty and delicious
Then full of thought
Now inside . . . as "That"
Now distinguishing again

Where is the chopping block?
My neck is drawn
Like lovers
To the Union

Beloved Self
Be merciful to what's left of me

Finish the job you started
With one beautiful swinging arc of the blade

There . . . now rolling to the ground
A severed head
And its dreamer

What is left?
Just this . . .

The sun shining through
An empty mind

Notes

Ambushed

They say
We have free will

But how free is the will
When on the way to the evening's meal
The moth meets the light?

When on the way to the tavern
The drunkard tastes the True Wine
He loses all interest in the old goblet

When ambushed by God
Thoughts of free will disappear

Only bats flying in the dark
Talk of free will
When the Light of God appears
You're too happy to worry about such things

The Love-Heart opens
You fall on your knees
The joy of finding The Self
Is inexplicable

The tears of Union flow
And you no longer worry
Which road to take

Notes

Isn't It Wonderful?

Isn't it wonderful
This magic
This laughter
This love madness for life

God sees Itself
Becomes delirious
With laughter

Love melts all

Praise the day
I entered this tavern

Notes

Sea of Presence

Mind
Is too small
A place to live

With its doer
And its constant fixing

Where did it ever
Get the idea
That things shouldn't be
The way they are?

The joys of thinking
Are not enough
Any more

The ocean
Has lured me away

Content now
To drown in the sea of Presence

Where . . .
There is nothing to do . . .
Except . . . perhaps . . .
To say "yes"

Notes

In the Here & Now

How can this be?

I'd like to meet
Whoever wrote this script
And got me
To play this role

They must be very funny
Probably howling somewhere
Or
Shedding a tear

I can't tell anymore

They hand me the script
As I go on

That's the way it is
In the here and now

Notes

From I to You

I leapt from I to You
And You devoured me

Yet here I am
Not an I at all

Notes

What a Ruckus

What could be better
Than writing poetry?

The doors flung open
Love streaming through
No one home to worry
About whether the bugs get in

What a ruckus
Loud music
Everyone dancing
Heads rolling

This ecstasy
Devours me
As an hors d'oeuvre

Then things really
Get rolling

Notes

Sweet Blasphemy

Looking everywhere
For God?

Try the place
You have overlooked

The place
So present
So obvious
So blasphemous

The place
The world has convinced you
It could never be

Try . . . yourself!

Notes

Never Have I Been So Drunk

I am a cup
Being passed
Among masters

Each one
Takes a sip
Until I am empty

It's getting low now

Ramana swallowed the separate one
Papa, the terror of annihilation
Gangaji, control

Now the cup empties of judgement
With a single story

Never have I been
So drunk
On so little

Never has this tavern
Looked so bright

Never have I been
This crazy
And so close
To the edge of the roof

Notes

Gentle as a Lover

Gentle as a lover
My Soul is

A whisper, a nudge
Now here, now there
Revealing the way
In silent gentleness

The ideal lover!
Love guiding itself

But turn a deaf ear
Or wander off into the brush
And the sound of the blade
Leaving the scabbard
Is deafening

This lover
Powerful as a samurai
Enters

Face to face
With the will of God
Horns lowered
Blade drawn
I see her wisdom

Gently
Garland with flowers
Or broken and bloodied
I return to the path

Notes

J Hear the Call

The window
Is closing
On this reality

I'm being called
Elsewhere

Gentle discontent
Now
A firmer voice
Later

When the soul
Wants you
Some other place
It has its ways

All that was right
Empties of brightness

Come gently like a lover
And you live the great adventure

Dally
And watch your world
Fall apart

When the breast moves
The baby must follow

Notes

No Time to Take a Nap

I have felt this boredom before!
It has the whisker marks
Of my Soul
All over it

My Soul says
"Keep moving
This is no time to take a nap
There is work to do
Follow the brightness
Of your Being
It will not fail you"

I'm sorry my love
I am being called elsewhere
On urgent business
I have no idea what it is

I can smell the Light
My Being wants it like a lover

Notes

Shiva Wouldn't Say

I should have asked Ram
About this
Before I came here

Shiva wouldn't say . . .
He just grinned

Now I'm here
Being dismantled
One sip at a time

It's getting brighter
As I disappear

I thought
I would become enlightened
What a joke!

My immolation
Is the light

I'm going to spank that Ram
If I ever find Him again
Unless I die laughing first

Notes

Satsang

I'm sorry . . .
But did you
Have a thought
Just then?

Yes . . .well . . .
You missed it!

We are traveling
The other way

Follow the thought
Backwards to its source

What you will find there
Is why we are all smiling

Notes

Hanuman Says to Ram*

So . . . Hanuman says to Ram

If I drown in You
I will be You

Not just yet!

Loving you
And drinking in your wine
Is too great a thrill
To drown just now

*For Justin

Notes

I Am the Last to Know

When your life
Gets up and leaves
You best follow

Yes I hear Your call
Silently
Requesting my presence
Elsewhere

You have come to me
Like this before
You lead
And I follow

If I deny you
You kill me:
Withering in Your absence
A death of starvation

If I follow
We rejoice together

Where are we going?
I am the last to know

At the Foot of the Third Millennium

The only way through all of this
Is to turn around
And face
The Nameless

There . . . in the silence
Your very Being
Awaits your presence

This love affair
Will end in a different kind
Of checkmate:

Your surrender
To the Presence of God
As yourself

So juicy!

This is not lofty philosophy
This is practical survival tactics
For living happily
At the foot of the third millennium

Notes

Falling Through

A lifetime
Of walking
On this pack ice

Now I've
Fallen through

It's warm
And loving

Notes

The Sage & the Wizard

She asked "Well ... are you in control?"
She was speaking to the redhead
But she was talking to me

Oh my God! I was naked
Everything collapsed

I wasn't in control!
Had never been in control
Would never be in control

It was so obvious
How had I missed it?

The magician inside
Groaned
I could hear tears pooling
In my wizard's eye

I had tried
My God I had tried

Yet it was so obvious
No ... I am not in control
Nor was I ever

I couldn't believe I had missed it
What was I doing all those years?
Intention, visualization, thoughts creating reality
But now ... who's reality?

Continued

Notes

The sage and the wizard had met
The wizard laid down his wand
And only the sage remained

Notes

Who Controls?

Think
You are in control?

Check again

Look in the back seat
At your boy
There . . . in the car-seat
The one with the plastic steering wheel

See him lean into the corners
Appearing to direct the motion
With the plastic wheel

Do you recognize anyone?
It's a mirror, my friend
You are looking at yourself

Who controls your life?
Take a good look

It's not the one
In the back seat
With the plastic wheel
In his hand

Notes

For Being Herself

Judgements come
Dropping their clothes
At my feet

A hot fog
Of forgetfulness
Lifts

How could I have been
So stupid
As to have an opinion
On such matters?

Naked for the first time
I see what I have done
Whipping God
For being Herself

I would die
For causing such pain
But God comforts me instead
Gives me a new set of clothes

And says
"Try not to shred them this time"

Notes

The Fall of Judgement

If I am not in control
Of my actions
My friend
Then you are not in control of yours!

And if you are not in control of your actions
How can I call you my enemy
When you act against me
Or judge you at all?

You must be as you are
As I must be as I am

God Herself is playing all the roles here

Perhaps I should just love Her
Wherever I see Her

Notes

The Open Secret

What could be
More obvious

Who is looking
Is what you are
Looking for!

Who is looking
Is the great mystery

So obvious
Once seen

So elusive
When thought about

Notes

Without an "I"

How is poetry written
Without an "I?"

There is no "I"
Inside me
No "me" inside this seer
Yet this poetry comes

A vast empty field
Of perception
Pervades
Is fullness itself

Pomegranates
Ripen

I had nothing
To do with it

Notes

The Search

This is your predicament

You are a fish
Born in the Sea
Looking for the Sea

How to tell you
That you are already in It

Would you give up the search
For one moment
And take a look
For yourself

You are so luminous
Only the mind could miss it

Notes

Because You Tell Stories

You suffer
Because you tell stories
Then believe them

You make things into
What they are not

I am this
She is that
It never ends

A thought arises
You bridle it up
And ride off on it

If you could just notice it
It would liberate itself
And disappear into whence it came

But no!
You saddle it up
Ride off

And your suffering
Is guaranteed

Notes

It All Happens in Silence

Life
Is lived in silence

Listen . . .
Do you hear any noise?

"Just the voice in my head"
You've listened to that for so long
You think it's normal

Wean yourself of that talking
Find the stillness
That lies beneath

Stillness is always there
The silent backdrop of life

That silence beckons
With the warmth of an open heart

It is all happening
In silence

Notes

Is This One, Is This Two?

Resting in myself

Feet propped up
Sipping tea
Looking out over the pond

Peace inside
Peace outside

Is there a difference?

Notes

Collision with the Infinite

Once a beggar
I shook my alms bowl
At every Saint
Where is God . . . Where is God?

They pointed
But I only saw
The finger

This headlong search
Ended in a head-on collision
"Call off the search" he said
"What you are looking for . . . is who is looking"

Looking within for this . . . "who"
There was . . . just . . . nothing
In that nothing-ness . . . silence
Beneath that . . . stillness

Oh my god!
This?
But this has always been here!

Exactly!

Notes

On Loving a Woman...

A few love poems are included here.

Love is our nature.
Love is to Self as wetness is to water.
What a great pleasure to love. To feel that beauty
flowing from the chest.

Others often act as the object that sparks that love
within us. The heart instinctively goes out to "the
other." Becomes fullness itself. We become alive with
our own loving. What deliciousness!

These poems are about loving a woman. And how the
"other" ignites that love craziness in the Heart . . . and
can drive you a little nuts. It's not always how you
would like it. Yet as you understand, you embrace
whatever arises. It comes, you know not why. You don't
judge it. It goes, you know not why. You don't ask
empty questions. You take what comes and experience
it all.

Whatever arises you will experience it, regardless how
beautiful or ugly. You function from the present
moment knowing you don't have the scope to judge any
of it. Life lives itself through you, as you. And you no
longer get in the way.

Notes

Just Let Me Love You

Just
Let me
Love you

It won't hurt

And you are
So beautiful

No behavior required
No change of plan needed
No expectation forthcoming

This Heart
Loves you

Let us both
Enjoy it
As One

Notes

Love

I have loved you
From the moment
I looked into your eyes
Across that silent table

Your soul . . .
I have no words
For what it does to me

I love you openly
Even now
And it will go on

That I can't be with you
Aches inside
That you are called elsewhere . . .
I fall to my knees
Then the tears begin

There is a love switch
Deep inside us
If I could reach it and turn it off,
Would I?

I turned to find it
When you told me

I locked it open!

Whoever bears this pain
Will have to cry these tears

Notes

Why?

Why?

I don't know why!

I know what is happening . . .
But I love anyway

I feel like a fool
I love anyway

I hurt
And I love anyway

Who are you
That makes me love like this?

That makes me a hero
In my darkest hour

Notes

Surrender

I would run
If I could
They are holding my feet

I would throw
The switch on oblivion
But they are keeping the lights on

Who is it
That is living here
Anymore?

I would surrender my life
But you took it
Years ago

Just hold my hand
As I cry

Notes

It Was Her Heart All Along

The Goddess
Appeared within me
Touched my Heart

It was Her Heart
All along

Now a flower grows there
Blooming . . . love

This garden
In me
As me

Notes

Love Is What Opens

You fly by
And these poems
Begin again

It must be
That love
Is what opens this mouth

My Soul does back flips
When it hears your voice
Like a dog
Happy to see its master

I tell It
"There are many fish in the sea
Don't worry over a small perch
In a random cove."

My soul has long ago
Stopped listening to me
What wisdom!
I think I'll follow suit

Notes

Huge Love

You got me
With that line
About "Huge love . . . is here for you"

The doors
Went flying by
That open to the Heart Cave

The cave was gone too
And the mountain

But not this feeling
Everywhere . . . Love

Notes

True Lovers

This love
Knows no bounds
It comes like a warm wind

If your Heart is open
This love will flow
Between us
Like a Holy river

If you stay
This love
Will consume us
A sacred feast!

If to another nest
You fly
This love shall go with you
Comforting, nurturing

So it is
With True Lovers

Notes

Invisible Food

Love . . .
That invisible food
God feeds on

Made by Itself
For Itself

The open Heart
Can't be seen
The ecstatic food It makes
Nourishes everything

Notes

Gear by Gear

I wasn't fortunate enough
To lose the whole transmission

It's being taken apart
Gear by gear

Now the high gear
Now low
The mid range
And overdrive

There goes the shifter
And the knob

The engine is next
I suppose
Then the chassis
And the seats

They will get to me
Soon
Then these poems
Will really take off

Notes

The Elephant

It's happening again
This tearing in the chest

It's not love this time
But that elephant
That comes visiting

My chest is ripped open

No words
Can touch it
But it's all
I want to talk about

All night
This happens
Then he lumbers off
In the morning

I am left with huge eyes
And a vast empty fullness
Blowing through
The chest

Notes

No Need for the Doors

Oh Heart
Open wide as the Self

Let me help
Take the hinges
Off the doors

No need for the doors
Anymore
No need for the wall
Either

Let this loving
Rush through

A constant
Pouring out from the Heart
A warm wind
Embracing life

No need for the doors
Or the walls

Just a wild hot wind
Rushing through
Where this house once was

Notes

Say What Can't Be Said

Longing . . .
Longing to say God
In poems

Praying
"String these words
Into a necklace
That sings Your beauty"

These pearls
Are in my mouth
Only You
Can speak them

Drop me to my knees
Say "You are All"
That "All is One"
Say "There is only God . . . and thou art that"

Say what can't be said
Here is Your hand
At the end of my arm

Say Yourself
To Yourself

Notes

Everything... You !

This craziness comes
And all I want to do
Is praise You

Every tree
Every cloud
Every smile
You!

The color blue
The scent of flowers
This feeling

Everything... You!

Notes

The "I" That Is Supposed to Be Here

If there is an "I" in here
Then it rests in the inner presence
That silent aware . . . something
That defies definition

Every "thing"
Takes its life from That

That Presence
Is all I can find!
I can't find this "I"
We all talk about

Can you ?

Ask the ancient question . . . "Who am I?"
Go on a hunt for that "I"
It leads right to The Presence

But try to describe It
It can't be touched with words
It's certainly not an "I"
It's far beyond that

And It loves . . .

Notes

Enlightenment

Enlightenment . . .
Allow it to be a mystery

The mind
And its ego
Never become enlightened

The separate one
Simply gives way
To something else

Like sugar dissolving in water
The mind and its separateness
Dissolve into the Being
That has always been the backdrop of your life

If you want to be enlightened
Dissolve into the silence
Of your Being

Then . . . no desire for enlightenment
Just the vast silent fullness
Of the Self

You have always been This
Sat - Chit - Ananda

Notes

Let It Love Itself Wildly

Spontaneous praise
Takes flight from the Heart
To the Sacred One

So exquisite

If there were anyone here
They would have to be
Very drunk

This awareness
Loves itself
So much

Don't stand in its way
Entranced by thought
Imagining it's you

Let it
Love itself
Wildly
As you

Notes

Stay as You Are

Vulnerable . . .
Living in the unknown . . .
That's the life
We awaken to

The Presence
Experiencing Itself
Living a life
As a human being

What is to come?
Who knows!

The mind would
Make you separate
And gift you with control

What an illusion!
Don't touch that rascal
And its dubious gifts

Stay as you are
As you really are

Pure silent awareness

Notes

Where Indeed!

Where am I from?

Not from
Where you think

Not from creation
At all . . .

From-ness
Lives here,
But I am
Not that

The I that is here
Is a vast emptiness
Full of light

Notes

Thirsty Friends

Once
I was a thinker

How did I ever
Endure it?

Thoughts arise now
But there is very little interest

How did I live
With such thirsty friends

I practiced Presence
For years
Then I saw
Who was present

Now I do nothing
And everything gets done

Notes

The Great Mystery

What a great laugh
Bubbles through life

That which appears substantial
Is in fact insubstantial

While that which seems so insubstantial
Is completely substantial

Not an ear can hear it
Nor eye see it
No hand has ever touched it

Dear friend
It is the very *space of you*
That is holy

Notes

Pristine Stillness

A winter's morning
Crisp and clear
Two feet of new snow
Silence . . .
Not a movement . . . anywhere

A pristine stillness
Lays across the land

This stillness
Greets me as I wake each morning
Follows me all day
Puts me to bed at night

Falling inward
I meet my Self
Pristine stillness

Notes

What Can't Be Let Go

Let everything go . . .

What is left
Is what can not be let go of:
The silent stillness
Of your True Nature

Content comes and goes
Thoughts come and go
What is it that does not come and go?

Circumstances come and go
States of consciousness come and go
What is the backdrop
That never comes nor goes?

Let it all go . . .
Then . . . see what is left

What is left is . . . consciousness
That which perceives
The Self

What is left is . . . you
You *are* That

Notes

Wake Up! Wake Up!

You slept through your teens
You did not wake up
You were playing at life

You slept through your twenties
You were having relationships

You slept through your thirties
The career was intense
You had to get somewhere
Make something of yourself

Now are you going to
Let the forties slip by
Sleeping the whole middle away?
Is your success that important?

Wake up!   Wake up!
The long night is over
Wipe the sleep from your eyes

A new lover is at hand
Calling silently
From your chest

Notes

The Hummingbird

The hummingbird
Is at the feeder
Drinking her fill
In the morning light

There is a silence inside
Undisturbed by thought
An ocean of silent Presence

I drink there

This sea of stillness
Is my nectar

The hummingbird
Drinks her fill
I am her
Drinking in the ocean

Soaking in this nourishment
I am my Self

Notes

Like a Cat

Like a cat
Curled up on the lap of God

I rest in That

Silence piles up
Like drifting snow

Stillness
Thick and rich
Enters my being

That which a moment ago I was
I am not
No longer the cat
But the lap

Notes

The Great Barrier

Yes
You have stumbled upon
The great barrier
And the gate
And the key to it

There . . .
In the stillness

Notes

What The Mind Can Not Know

At some point
The mind realizes
That it is not going to grasp it

That the Truth
Is so much larger
Than it is

The mind relaxes
Into what is
It gives up
And simply rests in the moment . . . as is

Bingo . . . awareness . . . presence
Did nothing . . . and there It was!
Silent, empty, a spacious vastness
The backdrop of every "thing"

Could it be
That it has only been thinking
That has obscured
This ever-present Wonder

Notes

Living Sages

currently giving Satsang in North America
in "non-dual" teachings (advaita)

Gangaji: Gangaji Foundation
505-A San Marin Drive, Suite 120, Novato, California 94945
(800) 267-9205 www.gangaji.org

Catherine Jngram: Dharma Dialogues
P.O. Box 10431, Portland, Oregon 97210
(503) 246-4235 www.dharmadialogues.org

Eli Jaxon-Bear: Leela Foundation
P.O. Box 936, Stinson Beach, California 94970
(415) 868-9800 www.leela.org

Hanuman
105 18th Ave #7, San Francisco, California 94121
(415) 221-5428 (fax) e-mail to: RamanaOne@aol.com

Mira
Brussels, Belgium c/o friends in Berkeley, California
(510) 524-2921 www.poonja.com/mira.htm

Eckhart Tolle: Freedom from Time Seminars
310 Tsawwassen Beach Road
Delta, British Columbia, Canada V4M-4C9
www.namastepublishers.com

Ramesh Balsekar
10 Sindhula, N. Gamadia Road, Bombay, India 400026

Francis Lucille: Truespeech Productions
Middletown, California (707) 987-2276 e-mail to: lucile@telis.org

Amber Terrell
Boulder, Colorado (503) 297-2181 / (760) 632-8872

Mary Margaret Moore
Santa Fe, New Mexico (505) 954-4788 e-mail to: justin.moore2@gte.net

Wayne Liquorman (Ram Tzu): Advaita Fellowship
P.O. Box 911, Redondo Beach, California 90277
(310) 376-9636 www.advaita.org

Byron Katie: The Work Foundation
P.O. Box 667, Manhattan Beach, California 90267
(877) 584-3967 www.thework.org

Nick Arjuna Ardagh: Living Essence Foundation
P.O. Box 2746, Grass Valley, California 95945
(530) 478-5985 and (888) VAS-TNESS www.livingessence.com
(very good web site with links to everyone)

Isaac Shapiro
Byron Bay, Australia
www.geocities.com/Athens/Thebes/2689 home.html

Satyam Nadeen: New Freedom Press
P.O. Box 3029, San Rafael, California 94912
(415) 457-3535 e-mail to: alchoice@ix.netcom.com

John de Ruiter: Oasis Edmonton
P.O. Box 78029, RPO Callingwood
Edmonton, Alberta, Canada T5T-6A1
(403) 487-8781 www.compusmart.ab.ca/truth

Adyashanti: Open Gate Sangha
P.O. Box 782, Los Gatos, California 95031-0782
(408) 236-2220 www.zen-satsang.org

Neelam: Fire of Truth Satsanga
Office: Ojai, California (805) 649-2272
Berkeley, California (510) 524-7730
www.neelam.org

Carlos Lopez
Boston, Massachusetts (781) 860-8930

Penny Whillians
Victoria, BC Canada (250) 385-0323
e-mail to: pjwhillians@home.com

Resources

If you have enjoyed these poems, you may find the following books & resources helpful:

WAKE UP AND ROAR: Volumes 1 & II *H.W.L. Poonja (Papaji)*
Pacific Center Publishing, P.O. Box 818, Kula, Maui, Hawaii 96790

THE TRUTH IS *H.W.L. Poonja (Papaji)*
Yudhishtara, P.O. Box 310, Huntington Beach, California 92648

BE AS YOU ARE: The Teachings of Sri Ramana Maharshi *David Godman*
Arkana/Penguin Group

YOU ARE THAT: Volume I & II *Gangaji*
Gangaji Foundation
505-A San Marin Drive, Suite 120, Novato, California 94945
(800) 267-9205

GANGAJI *Gangaji*
Cassette and video tapes of satsang (excellent)
Gangaji Foundation
505-A San Marin Drive, Suite 120, Novato, California 94945
(800) 267-9205

I AM THAT *Nisargadatta*
Acorn Press, P.O. Box 3279, Durham, North Carolina 27715

CONSCIOUSNESS SPEAKS *Ramesh Balsekar*
Advaita Press, Redondo Beach, California
(310) 376-9636 www.advita.org

COLLISION WITH THE INFINITE *Suzanne Segal*
Blue Dove Press, P.O. Box 261611, San Diego, California 98196
(619) 271-0490

THE POWER OF NOW *Eckhart Tolle*
Namaste Publishing Inc., P.O. Box 62084
Vancouver, British Columbia V6J-1Z1 Canada
(604) 943-7155 e-mail: namaste@bc.sympatico.ca

THE EASE OF BEING *Jean Klien*
Acorn Press, P.O. Box 3279, Durham, North Carolina 27715

SURPRISED BY GRACE *Amber Terrell*
True Light Publishing, P.O. Box 17734, Boulder, Colorado 80308

RELAXING INTO CLEAR SEEING *Arjuna Nick Ardagh*
P.O. Box 2746, Grass Valley, California 95945

BARTHOLOMEW *Bartholomew*
Cassette tapes available (excellent). Recommend monthly "Albuquerque talks" from August '92 onward and the last 6 retreats.
c/o Phyllis Johnson (keeper of the Bartholomew library)
P.O. Box 1414, Rancho de Taos, New Mexico 87557

I COME AS A BROTHER *Bartholomew / Mary Margaret Moore*
High Mesa Press, P.O. Box 98, Taos, New Mexico 87571

DOING NOTHING *Stephen Harrison*
Jeremy P. Tarcher-Putnam, New York

ONIONS INTO PEARLS *Satyam Nadeen*
New Freedom Press

THE ENLIGHTENED HEART: An Anthology of Sacred Poetry *Steven Mitchell*
Harper & Row, New York

THE ESSENTIAL RUMI *Coleman Barks & John Moyne*
Harper

**SAY I AM YOU; OPEN SECRET; RUMI: WE ARE THREE;
DELICIOUS LAUGHTER; BIRDSONG & UNSEEN RAIN: Rumi poems**
Coleman Barks & John Moyne
Maypop Books, Athens Georgia (404) 543-2148
Threshold Books, Putney, Vermont

THE KABIR BOOK *Robert Bly*
Beacon Press, Boston, Massachusetts

AUTOBIOGRAPHY OF A YOGI *Paramahansa Yogananda*
Self-Realization Fellowship Press, Los Angeles, California

CONVERSATIONS WITH GOD: Book 1 & 3 *Neale Donald Walsh*
G.P. Putnam Publishing Group, New York

THE SWORD OF NO-SWORD: Life of the Master Warrior Tesshu *John Stevens*
Shambhala Publications

About The Author

Born June 26, 1947, Chris McCombs grew up in Southern California, graduating from San Diego State University in 1969. It was a normal life for the place and times.

Then, in November of 1969, Chris had a vision that would change his life. He was 21 years old and had no previous religious interest. The war was on in Vietnam. He had been able to graduate at San Diego State by agreeing to become a Navy pilot after graduation. While training in T-34s at NAS Saufley Field in Pensacola, Florida, an unsolicited vision arose.

The vision raised the question, in a serious way, "What if there *really* were a God?" I mean, really were a God. And you could know Him directly. What then? This question had never come up before. But his gut response was: ". . . Well, if there really were a God, then I would want to know Him! Yes, I want to know the Truth."

In the language of Joseph Campbell, Chris had heard "the call" and was responding to it. A series of events quickly unfolded. The base commander called a meeting of all the Aviation Officer Cadets currently in flight school and said: "Gentlemen, the Navy overestimated its need for pilots. We have too many. Anyone who wants to leave the program please do so now; you are free to go."

"I'll take a couple of years off and explore this God issue. If it's the truth, then I want to be involved. If it's not the truth, then I'll be ahead of the game by knowing it now!"

While processing out of the Navy, he borrowed a book by Hans Holtzer on ghost hunting from another cadet. The book mentioned Author Ford, a famous psychic from the 1920s who had helped Hans. On the drive back to San Diego, Chris purchased an Arthur Ford book. It seems Ford had, in turn, been helped by the yogi Paramahansa Yogananda. As Chris arrived back in San Diego, he learned there was a Yogananda hermitage just up the road in Encinitas. Two hours later, sitting with a monk at the Self-Realization Fellowship hermitage, he bought <u>Autobiography of a Yogi</u>.

"Two chapters into the book, my hair was standing on end: self-realization, enlightenment, living illuminated masters, reincarnation, levitation and miracles, not in the distant past, but all going on right now. I knew deep inside my being that this was true. My bones knew it was true! I had never heard of such things, and yet somehow I knew."

When he picked up old mail at his last address, there was a job offer for the winter from Sun Valley Property Management for the winter. He headed for Idaho with his K2s and the <u>Autobiography</u>. The longing for God had mysteriously appeared.

The blue packets began arriving from SRF on how to meditate, how to still the mind and sit in the vastness of silence. It was then that the challenge came.

Two months into meditation practice, a draft notice arrived from the Pasadena Draft Board with a reclassification to 1-A. Yogananda had declared that anyone who sincerely prays to Babaji, the living immortal Yogi-Christ of India, would have their prayers answered. That night he went to sleep with the Autobiography beneath the pillow opened to Babaji's picture.

"I prayed: I don't want to go to war, I don't want to kill people, I want to find God. Help me avoid war and I will passionately search for God." And that is what happened. Three weeks later a 4-F notice (physically unfit for service) arrived unexpectedly from the same draft board. To this day, no one can explain how that happened.

Thirty years flew by: Kyria Koga, Meher Baba, Maharaji, Sufis, Sai Baba, traveling in India, Bubba Free John, EST, Actualizations, a career in real estate, aikido, Lazaris, Buddhism, Bartholomew, Rumi & Kabir, Papaji, Ramana Maharshi and Gangaji.

In June of 1997, everything flipped. *"The sense of entering the vastness, which had been discovered in meditation years ago, was gone. No one had ever entered it or left it. There was just no "one" there at all. That vastness was my Very Self. Nothing changed, yet everything changed."*

Chris lives on Orcas Island, Washington, writes poetry, and runs a business.

FANA PRESS

Delicious Silence
poems from the tiger's mouth

by
Chris McCombs

ORDER INFORMATION:

By Phone: (360) 376-7601 *or Fax:* (360) 376-2070

By E-mail: fana@rockisland.com

By Mail:

(*fill out form below and remit with check or money order to*: Fana Press at P.O. Box 667, Eastsound, Washington 98245-0667

Name ....

Address ....

City ....

State, Zip ....

Daytime Phone ....

Price per book: $12.95, $17.95 Canadian

Shipping & handling: $3.00 (first book), add $2.00 for each additional book

Total Enclosed ....